Color in My World

Orange Around Me

Madeline Stevens

Cavendish Square

New York

Published in 2015 by Cavendish Square Publishing, LLC
243 5th Avenue, Suite 136, New York, NY 10016

Library of Congress Cataloging-in-Publication Data

Stevens, Madeline, author.
Orange around me / Madeline Stevens.
pages cm. — (Color in my world)
Includes index.
ISBN 978-1-50260-067-7 (hardcover) ISBN 978-1-50260-069-1 (paperback) ISBN 978-1-50260-070-7 (ebook)
1. Orange (Color)—Juvenile literature. 2. Colors—Juvenile literature. 3. Color—Juvenile literature. I. Title.
QC495.5.S7486 2015
535.6—dc23
2014033132

9895

Editor: Andrew Coddington
Senior Copy Editor: Wendy A. Reynolds
Art Director: Jeffrey Talbot
Designer: Joseph Macri
Senior Production Manager: Jennifer Ryder-Talbot
Production Editor: David McNamara
Photo Researcher: J8 Media

The photographs in this book are used by permission and through the courtesy of: Cover photo by Daniel Grill/Getty Images; Fuse/Thinkstock, 5; chanwangrong/Shutterstock.com, 7; Laura Eisenberg/Getty Images, 9; ©iStockphoto.com/kickstand, 11; bbbrrn/iStock/Thinkstock, 13; justinecottonphotography/iStock/Thinkstock, 15; JLSnader/iStock/Thinkstock, 17; ©iStockphoto.com/BirdImages, 19; cbpix/iStock/Thinkstock, 21.

Printed in the United States of America

Contents

The world is full of orange.

Basketballs are orange.

Playing a game of basketball is fun!

Oranges are named for their color.

They are sweet fruit.

These oranges are **fresh**.

7

Some **vegetables** are orange.

These orange carrots
are vegetables.

They are **clean** and ready
to eat!

9

Pumpkins are another orange vegetable.

We make pumpkins into **jack-o'-lanterns** on Halloween.

11

Fire glows bright orange.

A safe fire can help us stay warm.

12

13

Many animals are orange.

This cat has orange **fur**.

He keeps his fur clean.

15

This puppy has orange fur, too.

Her fur is soft to pet.

This type of bird is called
an oriole.

He has bright orange feathers
on his chest.

18

19

Even fish can be orange.

This fish is called a clownfish.

He is easy to spot in the water!

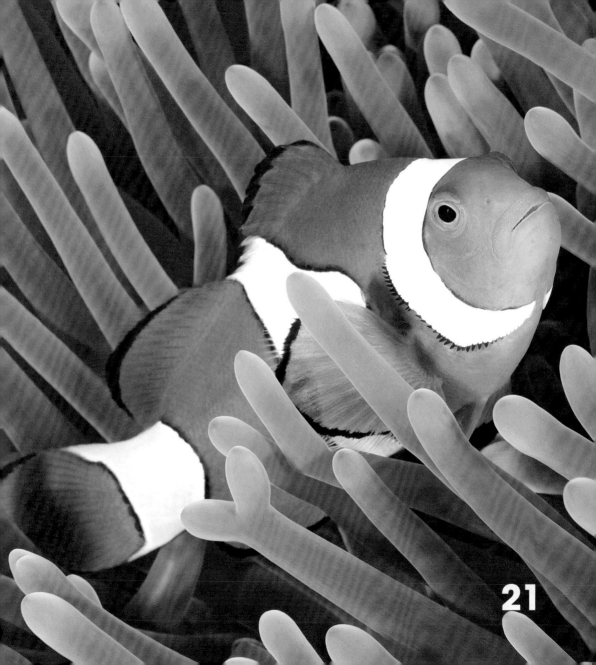

21

New Words

clean (KLEEN) Free of dirt.

fresh (FRESH) Newly gathered or made.

fur (FUR) The soft, fine hair on animals.

jack-o'-lanterns (JAK-o-LAN-turns)
Pumpkins carved to look like a face.

vegetables (VEJ-teh-bulz) Plants or parts
of plants used as food.

22

Index

23

About the Author

Madeline Stevens is a writer and former teacher. She lives in New York with her husband, son, and dog, Roxy.

About

Bookworms help independent readers gain reading confidence through high-frequency words, simple sentences, and strong picture/text support. Each book explores a concept that helps children relate what they read to the world they live in.